BLUES FOR UNEMPLOYED SECRET POLICE

poems by
DOUG ANDERSON

For my cousin Holly
good friend
and good soul

Doug Anderson

CURBSTONE PRESS

FIRST EDITION, April 2000
Copyright © 2000 by Doug Anderson
All Rights Reserved

Printed in Canada
Printed on acid-free paper by Best Book/Transcontinental Printing
Cover design: East Side Graphics

This book was published with the support of the Eric
Mathieu King Fund, the Connecticut Commission on
the Arts, and donations from many individuals. We are
very grateful for this support.

Curbstone wishes to thank Jane Blanshard and Barbara
Rosen for help in preparing this book.

Library of Congress Cataloging-in-Publication Data

Anderson, Doug, 1943-
    Blues for unemployed secret police : poems / by Doug Anderson.
    — 1st ed.
        p.   cm.
    ISBN 1-880684-70-5
    1. Vietnamese Conflict, 1961-1975 — Poetry. 2. Aging — Poetry. I.
Title.
    PS3551.N35848 B58 2000
    813'.54—dc21   99-462116

published by
CURBSTONE PRESS   321 Jackson Street   Willimantic, CT 06226
        phone: (860) 423-5110   e-mail: info@curbstone.org
                    http://www.curbstone.org

ACKNOWLEDGMENTS

My gratitude and deep affection to the MacDowell Colony where
some of these poems were written.

Some of these poems have appeared in the following
publications for which the author
gratefully acknowledges the permission to reprint:

The Alaska Quarterly Review
Field
Lilliput
The Massachusetts Review
The North Essex Review
The Other Side
Peregrine
The Virginia Quarterly Review

Special thanks to Gary Cordova, Fiona Spring, Jackie Sullivan,
and Al Wachtel.

Table of Contents

I
Blues

II
All of This

III

Homage to Neruda

IV

Answering Adorno

Blues for Unemployed Secret Police

I

BLUES

Blues

Love won't behave. I've tried
all my life to keep it chained up.
Especially after I gave up pleading.
I don't mean the woman,
but the love itself. Truth is,
I don't know where it comes from,
why it comes, or where it goes.
It either leaves me feeling the knife
of my first breath
or hangdog and sick
at someone else's unstoppable
and as the blues song says,
can't sit down stand up lay down pain.
Right now I want it.
I'm like a country who can't remember the last war.
Well, that's not strictly true.
It's just been too long.
Too long and my heart is like
a house for sale in a lot full of high weeds.
I want to go down to New Orleans
and find the Santeria woman
who will light a whole table full of candles
and moan things, place a cigar
and a shot of whiskey in front of Chango's picture
and kiss the blue dead Jesus on the wall.
I want something.
Used to be I'd get a bottle
and drink until the lights went out
but now I carry my pain around everywhere I go
because I'm afraid

I might put it down somewhere and lose it.
I've grown tender about my mileage
My teeth are like Stonehenge and my tongue
is like an old druid fallen in a ditch.
A soul is like a shrimper's net they never haul up
and it's full of everything:
A tire. A shark. An old harpoon.
A kid's plastic bucket.
An empty half-pint.
A broken guitar string.
A pair of ballerina's shoes with the ribbons tangled
in an anchor chain.
And the net gets heavier until the boat
starts to go down with it and you say,
God, what is going on.
In this condition I say love is a good thing.
I'm ready to capsize.
I can't even see the shoreline.
I haven't seen a seagull in three days.
I'm ready to drink salt water,
go overboard and start swimming.
Suffice it to say I want to get in the bathtub
with the Santeria woman and steam myself pure again.
The priest that blesses the water may be bored.
Hung over. He may not even bless it,
just tell people he did. It doesn't matter.
What the Santeria woman puts on it with her mind
makes it like a holy mirror.
You can float a shrimp boat on it.
The spark that jumps between her mind
and the priest's empty act
is what makes the whole thing light up

like an oilslick on fire against a sunset over Oaxaca.
So if I just step out into it.

If I just step off the high dive over a pool
that may or may not have water in it,
that act is enough
to connect the two poles of something
and make a long, blue arc.
I don't have a clue about any of this.
Come on over here and love me.
I used to say that drunk.
Now I'm stark raving sober
and I say, *Come on over here and love me.*

Babylon

Wear my feet off
    down to the knees in this city
        where everything's ground down to bone dust.

Weave of curse and love cry.
    Unhatched plots, foamy
        fomentations, so many mouthfuls

and so many watch-your-mouths.
    But here I am again
        wondering why

I want to come back
    to a place where tenderness
        is the moment between

the lion's last kill
    and a new appetite.
        You'd think a sane man

would move out to mall country
    where you can see all that sky
        in a woman's eyes

but I'm back here every year
    looking for something I've lost,
        where the park trees grow snake-hide

and the pigeons
        have great broken-knuckled feet.
            You can't keep me away.

I guess I need to be where the noise
        on the outside is equal to
            the noise on the inside,

otherwise I'd be an ambulance trapped in traffic,
                        siren rising.

II

Can't stop to figure;
        I'm too busy with all the
            eye music along the perfumed

crowd-thick crotch-funky block
        of hustlers and hustlees.
            Maybe there's a point to this,

like the money they burn
        down below in the Tartarean machinery,
            but I don't think so.

Someday we'll find out
        gold's just a pretext
            and all the flying elbows,

all the trying to stand
on one clod of real estate
are really love gone wrong.

There's something sweet
about all the fucked up good intentions,
all the bungling baksheesh kings

and outcast inspectors
jealous for the hot spot,
wheedling for bribes and rum babas

down here in the big concrete trough
that rolls the rainwashed blood
down to the river and out to sea.

But there's a raw heartbeat
in the ozone silence after the storm.
Why not spend the end of the world

at the world's end?
The meteor only comes alive
between the air's hard shell

and the blood black dirt.
That moment and no more.

Madonna

That day I rang the wrong bell
you answered the door bare breasted,
boa constrictor around your neck.
You thought I was the postman.
He was such a sad man, you said,
you put a little yeast in his mojo.

Come back, you said.
I brought you bouquets of iron roses,
a carved walnut stock for your mauser,
you sewed me a pair of eelskin pants, ah!
candlelit nights in your glass tub.
How you sang in that red satin bed,
your hair a corona of black fire.

Our love outlived the boa who died
from the frozen mice.

But then you started with the tarantulas,
producing them in the palm of your hand at parties,
trying to scare tenured professors to death,
bats brought back from Mexico on the Harley,
your hair an obsidian flame behind you.
After the incident with the blow darts, I left.

I joined the sons of Odin,
razors and horned helmets, always on the move.
I light candles for you
at every roadside shrine between Tucson and Nogales.

Now by the river, my feet in red water,
a salamander curls around a plaster madonna
like a sable stole. I feel your presence.
I say, it's a damn shame, love is.

Performance

We knew about the advertising executive who roller-skated
through the village dressed as Tinkerbell, and then there
was that couple with shaved heads who showed up at
everything wearing matching silver jump suits and chrome
World War I helmets, but the best was always unexpected
like my first day in town walking down Hudson near 14th
Street, I see this black guy in a white tux, white vest,
white shoes, holding a white telephone receiver, its white
cord coiled down into his fly. He is frozen in the posture of
a royal guard, phone held at the ready. I give him plenty of
room but when I pass him he smiles beatifically, thrusts
the receiver in my face and says: *It's for you: it's the
White House.*

The Visit

Death is strolling down the walk.
He passes the dog and the dog falls dead,
an up-ended piñata in the moon-luminous grass.
I am in the house packing.
I have film of my life in my sweaty hand.
Edited into sweet and awful.
Been told to pack light.
Where I'm going I'll get new things,
shoes will not be necessary.
Nor will books, condoms, waterclocks, bonsai.
The film is coiled in its can.
I play it back in my head.
Death ambles onto the porch.
The parrot swings upside down from rigored talons,
bright black eye frozen in its red circle.
Death stops to smoke.
I can hear the porch swing creaking.
Something's wrong.
The film has only moments of intensity,
nothing in between.
Death is a chain smoker.
He coughs. His zippo clinks and flares.
He's in no rush.
What was edited out of the film?
Down on my knees now looking
under the bed, grabbing at discarded bits
of celluloid
but they're all fragments. A shoulder. Pair of lips.
Like pieces of a Sappho poem
found on burnt papyrus from the library at Constantinople.

I put the clips together: a stream of images.
Death is up now and moving.
He enters the house. Goes to the ice-box for beer.
I hear him pop the top.
I hear the cat's strangled last breath.
Should I put on a suit?
Too late to change anything.
The best of me is probably on the out-takes.
Simple things. A rainy afternoon when I felt fine
in my own skin.
Not all the Wagnerian hoopla, the *grand mal* of love.
Death is on the stairs.
But when I look, he's not there.
He's left a note taped to the banister: *I'll be back.*
The cat revives in the kitchen.
The parrot says, *Fuck you, Jesse.*
And the dog
is barking at the shadows.
I crumple the note and toss it.
The lawn glows soft green.
I pick up pieces of film and hold them up to the moon.

Blues for Unemployed Mercenaries

For Martín Espada

*The Hole, Rikers Island. Stainless steel toilet, bunk,
surveillance camera up in the shadows; otherwise, the cell
is empty. A powerfully built man in early forties lit by soft
glow sits on bunk. Prison sounds in background. He
speaks:*

All I wanted was a goddam cab
and these two scumbags
had to say that thing about my hat,
I mean,
I was jet-lagged.
Hadn't been back from Joburg
two hours
these sorry fucks had to start:
Looka that hat. Whaddya work in a bathhouse?
Get me a towel, boy.
Then, heat-lightning,
snake-brain
to fingertips: I been trained.
Didn't even
take the time to love it,
my forty dollar hat
right down that guy's throat.
First thing here
got me another Turk hat
off a Muslim.
Word was out.
Nobody said nothin'
bout my hat. No
body. In the chow hall

guy looks at me
I say, You like my hat?
and he looks down.

Didn't say
I like your hat a whole lot
or
Your hat is positively chic
'cause he had a notion
I'd put my fork
through his adam's apple,
knew what to do;
not like these sorry fuck tourists,
reason I'm here.
Come through the trap
when I got here,
Chicom shrapnel in my ass
sets off the metal detector,
Guard says
I hear you like hats,
you wanna try to wear mine,
you fuck?
and they got me shackled
wrist to ankle
or I woulda rearranged
his chromosomes.
And then they strip search me
as if I'm dumb enough
to have contraband up my ass.
Went down to the yard,
parted the waters,
just walked through
and they stood aside

except for Mohammad
and his black ass is glad to see me
even if I am
an ice bullet man—'scuse me—
paramilitary consultant.
Fuckin' Afrikaners
never could get it right,
always too quick to load.
You don't take
the bullets out of the freezer
till the last,
keep some guys firing rubber bullets
till your snipers
can pick out the politicals
from their pictures,
then you load the ice
and drop the fuckers
and they haul them off to the morgue,
screaming,
I saw dem shoot, mon, I saw dem.
But when they cut 'em open
guess what melted
in all that blood and body heat.
Pick up my check and go to Bangkok,
shave my beard,
blend in with all the software salesmen
on a pussy hunt
and pretty soon I'm back in the world
except those sorry tourist fucks
had to say that about my hat
and now I'm in here.
I wish Yehuda would

get me out of here.
Don't care what I have to do
for him afterwards,
I mean, I'm a professional.
Worked for Pinochet.
I'll even work for NSA.
Anything but here.
Mother come by yesterday,
saw my picture in the paper.
Hadn't seen her for 10 years.
Sits down and starts to cry.
Says, *I raised you Christian*
and you come back from that war
meaner than a landlord.
I said Mama, in Pakistan
they take orphans and break
their legs
before they send them out to beg
and the people
who take their money at the end of the day
go home to fine houses.
That's the kind of world it is, Mama.
Yehuda's gonna get me out
and I'm gonna
take you to a French Restaurant,
show you what kind of money
an ice bullet man makes.
By the way, you like my hat?

Blues for Unemployed Secret Police

They know deep down
how goes the world.
The dangerous then
are the dangerous now.
Stop shaking,
I know these border guards,

A surgeon's scented hands,
pale green eyes,
mustache cropped and waxed
turns up one corner
when he smiles: *My tie on straight?*

Let me do the talking.
My God, woman, stop crying,
put on your shades,
you look like a harlequin.

He's good at embassy parties,
takes in the whole room,
a nod stage left, stage right,
makes you feel as if
you've always known him,
could touch him for a buck
if things got bad.
His wife is good with children,
chairs four charities,
has lovely daughters
whose interlocking marriages
would, were there still a state,

bring him close to royalty,
but this is not to be.
Already new tyrants' faces
appear on higher bills,
make bribery complex.
What an awful thing to happen
to this nice family.
Woman, stop whining,
do something with your face.
The helicopter's waiting in the marsh.
He has friends, besides,
who anticipate his needs,
for whom he'll do the same. *And besides,*
they'll be looking to hire know-how.
Get out the photo albums of the old regime,
update my résumé, do something
with the bloodstains on my suit.
And did you pack the special files? Already
the rabble's disemboweling arms grow tired.
Have they stopped shooting lawyers yet?

Dear Wife, you've lost your faith in faithlessness.
A good torturer can always find a job.

Ars Poetica Blues

The world
and its counterweight
silence. How
a shout brings up flesh.
Don't even
call them mysteries,
call them facts.
Like the filament of blood
where scalpel
touches skin
and the baby is
swung by its ankles
over the wound.
Like the fact of rain
or the burnt honey
of her neck.
Sometimes
when I sing
I feel the word
drag its rusty anchor
through the muck.
Get me ignorant again.
Take me back
to the stammering place.
Shuck me
of words that slide
too easily.
I want to tell you
I'm so simple
I could be you.

Can you love
somebody
trailing his harpoons,
old ropes rotted
to rags in the wake?
I tell you Death
makes me sweeter.
Bring me everything
on the menu.
Give away my complications
and sell
everything else.
These are final
wishes. I forgive
everybody with a soul.
Tell my old lovers
I meant it
when I was there.
Words are so much swamp gas.
Why didn't I
learn something useful?
I used to fly in my sleep,
used to glide over
the old neighborhoods.
In those dreams
I knew where the money
was buried,
where the mojo
rose in the dark.
Look at me naked
and bent kneed
in nothin' but my reptile brain

naming things.
This hairy old heart says
water. Says salt.
Says stone.

New Woman Blues

Inside my white armor I am covered with hair and lice.
I haven't bathed for so long I no longer stink
but give off the odor of perfumed catacombs.
When I open my mouth to say I love you
spiders run over my lower lip and down into my beard.
There is a mouse tail hanging out of the corner of my mouth.
I want our first moments alone to be messy.
I want you to feel all the terror of me you will ever feel, now.
If you take me as I am I will never disappoint you.
I wake at night and cut my dreams into paste-ups;
the snack snack snack of the scissors will test you.
I am violent and unpredictable.
I eat snake heads.
I have invited my beast to come live in my skin,
look out through my eyes.
I deny nothing.
I have no secrets.
I will give you more truth than you ever wanted.
I fuck like the last day on earth.
When your parents come to visit
I will lead them into the room which is always in darkness
and there under the black light
show them my collection of missionaries
from all over the world.
When I say I love you
great greased cogs begin to turn
down below the sewers.
With me you have always more than you wanted.
Your leprosy is nothing to me.
Your psychotic episodes,

your collection of Filipino war knives,
nothing; your vibrating bras
ringed with Italian Christmas lights,
nothing compared to the vise-grip I'll put on your heart.
Your legs will shake so badly waiting for me to come home
you'll scarcely notice they get worse when I'm there.
I drink a glass of blood every morning.
The Jehovah's Witnesses will not knock on my door.
Now I've told you everything.
No surprises down the road, no disappointments.
I'm sorry I've done all the talking.
That's the hardest thing of all you'll have to bear.

History Blues

*The waters compassed me about, even to the soul:
the depth closed me round about, the weeds
were wrapped about my head. Jonah 2:5*

Those days
we scarcely bathed off the scent
of one lover before
tangling tongues with the next.
Now we're moving slow and steady
through whatever it is.
It's *mean,* we know that much.
Half the people have got Rotweilers,
the other half
are on leashes themselves.
You tell *me.*
But this day is fine.
Wind has blown away the smog
and somebody is burning sweet wood
in a fireplace.
I don't even mind the plastic Santa
someone stuck
in his front yard crèche, arms thrust out
like Jolson
kneeling before the Christ child.
Could be worse: we could have mortgages
extending into the next life, hearts packed in duckfat.
Instead, we just ripen, give off our sweet funk.
Death knows where I live.
So what. *I don't go to bed with nobody
don't know who Ho Chi Minh was.*
The Zohar

says the storm was Jonah's passion,
the whale his body,
and when he was spat out on the shores of Nineveh
he had the stain of being human,
was worth at least the weight of wet clothes.
Old friend, let's talk about
how our skins have moved on around us
like maps, how our scars
refract the light passing through us as we fade.

Lies

I am not so sure you are stewardess as you say.
I think you are a psychic terrorist,
uncommonly sweet, but you lift weights.
I have never loved a woman whose biceps, triceps,
trapezius, latissimus dorsi, deltoids, abductor, adductor
and, oh, your vastus internus,
so differentiate themselves, so glisten,
so move like slow-motion shot of an earthquake
through a stretch of desert.
I do not believe your degree is in metaphysics,
that you write children's animation films
during stopovers in Hong Kong, nor
that your father was shot down over Burma
in the Big War, and as a humanitarian gesture,
a tribal chieftain sent you his head.
I say, Liar, and how your eyes incandesce,
starfruit in deep amber, how your oiled hands
ply the plastic explosive thighs,
now stroking rictus muscle, down into
the fire that, unshaven, spills out of your pelvis,
appropriates the dunes, the iliac crests.
I ask your name and you begin to lick me,
say you need the salt—the heat, the heat.
The people around us begin to move away,
dragging blankets, radios, towels,
looking wistfully over their shoulders,
and now, as the night sky covers us,
my nerves radium bright,
I dismantle the constellations,
remake them into new lies,
send them spinning.

II

ALL OF THIS

All of This

For Jack Gilbert

The moist smell under the oleanders.
Water that has passed through pines.
Old bottles baked blue in hot sand
in the time I have been alive.
We don't come with souls, we make them up
out of our ripening and our going to seed.
The burnt musk of a lightening-struck oak.
The way women are borne up when they walk
even as the earth pulls them down.
The last cedar log and the winter
far from over. The willow's pale gold in autumn.
The smell of love on my fingers.
Coyotes who amble through town
in the dry season to drink from sprinklers.
The owl I surprised in the old ice house,
tall as a ten-year-old, widening its wings at me.
How someone I loved long ago shows up in my cells,
speaks through my mouth.
The way memory keeps safe under the wing
of forgetfulness. And the way
death is kinder to me now that I know his name.
All of this, and a longing that runs like a jackal
over a plane of mind so empty
it can hold everything, even as I forget myself in it.

Oedipus Blind

My eyes which are not there
move as I say this.
You should have known Jocasta.
She was like figs which lie
in the sun till the beads of nectar
come and the courtyard
fills with bees. When I first
came to her she slipped the tunic
from my shoulders
with one finger and looked at me.
The sweat pooling in my collarbones.
The pulse in my cock.
You cannot know what this was like.
The smell of her.

The Oracle

On the altar the flies of God
swarm on the pomegranates and roasted oxen.
We say we want to know the truth
but as the light sweetens
and the priestess does not arrive
we grow comfortable with the old lies.
I want and do not want the razor-edged
pendulum that swings in my heart.
The woman gone and why.
Years of wide-eyed blindness.
There is tenderness in all gathered here
in the shade of the temple.
When we were young we dreamed
of a plateau where everything
could be seen in all directions
and suffering evaporated in wisdom.
Silence is the power
that pools in the shadows of words
and when finally we stop speaking
it pins us to the ground

Between Passion and the Next Thing

When we cannot possibly make love again
I discover we are not alone in the silence.
The ghosts in this old house whisper advice.
This is where we blew it, they say.
This is what you must do now to avoid disaster.
Now that the great beast has quit thrashing
reel in the slack line.
But mostly they say, how well do you suffer?

Turning Fifty

This morning I swam out
into the cold
where the depths began,
turned back toward the young
people on the beach, shouting,
beautiful out here,
then felt the wind in my face
carrying my voice out
over the water like a lost scarf.

Morning

And the large stones in my head
coming to rest.
Birds. The old man across the street
starting his truck. In the mirror
my ghost becomes flesh part by part
with the assistance of light.
All night I have been pulling a heavy barge
by a rope in the black water.
The current helping a little towards dawn.

Light

She is telling me about a machine that creates light
for people in countries with desolate winters.
The mental and spiritual benefits thereof.
She is young and buoyant and I think she gives off light.
Even the scar on her lip is beautiful,
the way it makes her story hers and hers only.
Then the young man comes and smiles at her
and without speaking they go into the next room
where there are photographs
of terrible suffering and oppression.
Where she was sitting, a darkness sharp and deep,
like the cool blindness of a doorless Mexican bar
where you come in out of the white sun and it takes
time to be able to see the dim red lights.
As I go out I imagine her standing in front of the photographs
and the colors coming back into the black and white images
the way the blood has come back to my skin
or the way the pale green tips the gray branches
even now, in this cold of early March.

Itinerary

In Arizona coming across the border with dope in my tires
and for months tasting the rubber in what I smoked.
With a college degree and a trunk full of the war.
Working in one place long enough to get the money
to stay high for a month and then moving on. Drinking a quart
of whiskey, then getting up, going to work the next day.
A little speed to burn off the hangover. In the afternoon
A few reds to take the edge off the speed and then to the bar.
At the bar, the madonna in the red mirror. My arm around her
waist and the shared look that said: The World Is Coming Apart,
Let Us Hold One Another Against The Great Noise of It All.
Waking with her the next morning and seeing her older,
her three year-old wandering in and staring with a little worm
of confusion in his forehead. The banner on the bedroom wall
that read ACCEPTANCE in large block letters.
At night going out to unpack the war from my trunk.
A seabag full of jungle utilities that stank of rice-paddy silt
and blood. To remind myself it happened. Lost them somewhere
between Tucson and Chicago. Days up on a scaffold
working gable-end trim with Mexicans who came through
a hole in the fence the night before. Rednecks who paid
me better than them. Laughing at jokes that weren't funny
to keep the job. At a New Braunfels Oktoberfest getting in a fight
with a black army private who wore a button that read,
Kiss me I'm German. Don't remember what the fight was about.
Back in Tucson. Up against the patrol car being cuffed
for something I don't remember doing. Leaving the state.
Back with Jill in San Antonio. Finding her in the same bar,
driving her home in her car because she was too drunk.
The flashers on behind me and the flashlight in my face.

In those gentle days, they drove you home. Stealing Jill's car
out of the impound lot next day to avoid the fee.
Later sitting buck-naked across from one another at the breakfast
table wondering who we were. This woman who wanted to live
with a man who had dreams so bad he would stay awake for days
until the dreams started to bleed through into real time
and he had to go back the other way into sleep to escape them.
Who woke with the shakes before dawn
and went to the kitchen for beer. Later walking down
to the barrio slowly, without talking, our hips touching.
The Mexican restaurant, a pink adobe strung with chili pepper
Christmas lights the year round. Inside, the bullfight calendar
with the matador's corpse laid out on a slab, naked and blue
with a red cloth across his loins and the inevitable grieving virgin
kneeling at his side. The wound in the same place the centurion
euthanized Christ with his spear. Our laughing then not laughing
because laughter and grief are born joined at the hip.
An old Mexican woman fanning herself at the cash register,
her wattles trembling. *Recordar:* to remember, to pass again
through the heart. Corazón. Coraggio. Core.

In Heaven

The musicians have picked up hammers,
smashed their instruments, moved on
to other things, great copper pots, doll's heads,
urns of honey, bursting them with
single ecstatic blows, knowing that
happiness does not last. But, my love,
I love you even as we cool,
bells in a high winter wind, still
trembling under their gloss of frozen rain.

Kimono

She would come in the mornings and we would undress as soon
as she closed the door, cheeks cold from the Massachusetts winter.
Not much talking. We had two hours and if we were lucky, coffee
after. But I remember the importance of doing things in order.
Undress first, then kiss. The eyes open in this kiss, the whole body
kissing, a meld, a weld at the groin. The day changing without us
and the traffic building up in the street below. I kept a robe for
her, a cheap, cotton kimono, white with blue chrysanthemums so
faded they looked like the blurred shadows of the flowers on the
stucco wall. Too flimsy for winter, but her in it, putting up her
hair before the shower and her body flushed pink with love.
Careful not to get her hair wet, but the strawberry flush down her
neck into her full breasts remained. It would fade, she said,
during the long trip down the interstate. Her entering finally the
blue dark of her own house, picking up a toy, the mail, just inside
the door. Her gone and me with the rest of the day. The kimono
in the dark closet full of her smell.

Phan Thiet

For Thuy Le

You speak to me
of walking through the village
with your grandfather,
his slow ramble, your love
of all miracles equally
(the pigs the sugar cane the hanging ducks)
when suddenly he gathers you up
like a bundle of long stemmed flowers
and runs. Sputter of
automatic weapons behind you.
A scream. Before that,
inside your mother,
the shared blood pumping faster,
swelling your little heart.
Soldiers in the village
probing thatch with bayonets.
The kicked-over rice.
The family altar
scattered in the dirt.
And now when you take
the steaming tea
in both hands, for me
you are lifting the red cloth
from the mirrors,
letting memory pour into the room.
You look into the green well
of the teacup,
the warmth passing
through your fingers and into your eyes.

Frankfurt, 1972

A man and a woman lie in each other's arms
in a deep, open-eyed kiss.
They met at the airport and they could not
leave because of the snow, rented a room together
and made love the whole day.
And now, eye to eye, they wonder.
Deep in the old-fashioned feather bed,
steam pipes knocking in the walls
and a siren threading its way down Goethestrasse.
She weeps afterwards and he does not ask why.
He thinks, how many has he rubbed skins with
and called *Lover.*
His heart is too slow for the times,
lingers with the old lover
even when the body has gone on to the next.
And now he weeps too and she does not
ask why. Stares at the gargoyle
crouching on the building across the street
as if it might open
its stone wings and lift off into the swirling snow.

Return, Winter 1994

*The seat of the soul
is where the inside meets the outside*
— *Novalis*

This morning the old couple who live below
are playing a duet, trombone and piano,
botching it, stopping,
to laugh between disasters, then forging on.
I remember that summer in New York,
the Puerto Ricans next door on 12th Street,
their love cries echoing up the air shaft,
my solitude a cold star in that hot dark.
But these last years I have chosen what I always feared.
Enough rubbing skins together just to make a spark.
This time I wanted to listen to what lies below
the ache, below the pulse in the neck,
something uncommonly delicate,
entirely me or entirely God. Like the wild grapes
hidden in their leaves.
You are crowded in your own house,
the mirrors are full of you,
even your books give you back your own face.
You are everywhere, look,
how huge your hand with the spoon in it,
how loud your eating.
Your body fills the tub like a swollen corpse.
Now that you know your own holy noise
go where there are other bodies, let their smells overpower you.
Become small, one among many.

III

HOMAGE TO NERUDA

We Agree to Sleep for a Week

On the first night of our sleeping
as my eyelids began to tremble
she cut the web
that held us to the world
and we drifted past the city,
spike-spined in its hive of light,
single beacon blinking.
I let my hand drift in the water
beside our bed.
We passed the channel islands
with the bell no one could find.

On the second night of our sleeping
I stayed awake and watched her,
gave her a name, a self,
drew a map of her childhood
and in a fit of valor
killed her father with an axe.
Then I slept,
bed turning slowly in the current.
When I woke
we were tangled in cypress roots,
a hundred children
stared at us from the bank,
their tambourines silent.
I hacked the roots that held us
and we were free,
the river black glass and the stars
swirling in the eddies.

On the third night of our sleeping
she stayed awake while I slept,
axe in hand,
ear touching my lips,
listening for the names
of my old lovers.
We slid between the banks
where lightning had lit fires in the dry fields.

On the fourth night of our sleeping
we tied up
at an island of escaped slaves
who etched stick gods on rocks
with railroad spikes.
When we told them
we were not anthropologists
they fed us, bathed us,
cut holes in our heads
to let the evil out
so that we had to gather it back up
like mushrooms
to recognize ourselves.

On the fifth night of our sleeping
we were married
by a man or woman with a snake's head
in an undertaker's suit
who took our money,
slipped out of his skin
and went over the side
while we flopped on the decks
like sharks

hauled up with the shrimp.
By morning, your belly swelled.

On the sixth night of our sleeping
you gave birth
to a child with one blue eye and one brown,
who came out mumbling a phrase
in a language we'd never heard,
chanting,
as if to tell us something that would save us.

On the seventh night of our sleeping
the child stood at the rudder
while we hung our feet in the black water
and fought. You accused me
of seducing you,
I accused you of liking it.

And then I dreamed that we had wakened,
found you sleeping,
found you strange,
in fact, had never met you
nor you me
and yet this child at the rudder
and yet this bouquet of knives.

Coyote

Angle iron of darkness
crossing the road,
one eye on me   the other
on the bird you hoped for
but now
with empty jaw-clomp
gone.
You know me by my half-eaten sandwich,
no more,
after all,
we taught you
how to be in this world
of hunger by design,
so you nip at the edges
of the scene
our sentimental dog-love
would draw you into
that our children
might dig their fingers
into your thief's
flea-furious ruff.
Bat-eared
and moon-fanged,
your friends the crows
would love you
did they not lust
for the same road-kill.
You know us by
our desire
to eat the heart out of the world

and leave the rind,
so you have learned to cherish
crust and gobbet, cursed
and loved us
from the beginning,
yipped
from the tops
of the mountains
of garbage you share
with the gulls
(or the Tijuanan
who digs for cans
and for breakfast
stops to pluck
the unrotten part
from a rotten chicken).
Shoulder blades
just this side of wings,
road dancer,
poodle bandit,
drinker from the swimming pools
of those
who moved to the city's periphery
to escape their brothers.
We claim not to know you   you
are all we seek to hide,
and pretend
the numbers we punch in,
gates we lock,
mind-grates
we slide shut at the end of the day
(whose clanging

is the waking song of thieves)
are so many sounds
a good mixer
could smooth out
to give us
one serene,
lingering echo of the past.
But then you start
your singing at the edge of town,
mockery
your friends the crows
understand
from the ancient dialects of hunger.

Crows

Hunch in the trees
to gossip
about God and his inexorable
experimenting,
about deer guts and fish so stupid
you could sell them air
and how out in the deserts
there's a dog called coyote
with their mind
but no wings.
Crow with Iroquois hair.
Crow with a wisecrack
for everybody,
Crow with his beak
thrust through a bun,
the paper still clinging.
Then one says something
and they all leave,
complaining
the trees are not
what they used to be.
Crow with oilslick eyes.
Crow with a knife
sheathed in a shark's fin.
Crow
in a midnight blue suit
standing in front of a judge:
Your Honor, I didn't
kill him,
just ate him

and I wasn't impressed.
Crows
clustered in the bruise light
in the bottoms
of dreams.
Crows in the red maple.
Crows keeping disrespect
respectable.
Crows teasing a stalking cat,
lifting off at the last minute,
snow shagging down
from their wings.
Crows darkening the sky,
making fun of the geese
on their way to Florida.
Crows in the roses,
beaks and thorns.
Crows feeding lizards
to their brood.
Crows lifting off road kill,
floating back down
after the car has passed.
Crow with a possum eye
speared on its beak.
Crow with a French fry.
Crows
in the chicken cages
on their way to market,
the farmer
finally gone mad.
Crows hunkered down
rumpling feathers,

announcing the cataract
of snow
over the sun.
The crows prosper.
Carrion is everywhere.
The night
that is coming
is so dark
it will feel
like fur on the eyes.
So dark suddenly
you cannot see the snow.
Thrust your hand in it.
Hear it like sand
blowing on the roof.
A crow shifts his foot
and snow sifts
down from the tree.

Lizard

Shadow seared in stucco,
you were here at the beginning   your
sloughed skins,
lost tails,
decoys that imitate death,
eyes hooded arabs in the chalk light.
Your shadow a needle
blown from a furled tongue
so fast I'd miss it
were it not a razor of dark
in the burnt blind day   your feet
little acts of will on a wall.
Metaphysician
drawing the story of light
larger in each twirled telling.
Live petroglyph
banished long ago with the others   you fell
in millions, too light
to go all the way to the center,
graced the surface,
are content to stay.
Lizard in the broken porcelain bowl.
Lizard in the bathroom sink.
Lizard in the eaves   in the drawer,
you have been here always,
half-moon gaze steady on us   your
heart is pure honey,
I would break you open
like a ripe pod
and know everything and especially

death in his black box.
Lizard on the mirror   no,
on the wall.

Lizard where the faucet leaks
and leaves a pool
in the shade of the house,
pausing as my shadow passes over you.

Lizard who can go all week
on one quick, tongueful of rain.

Colonial Album

For Yusef

They saw mirrored
in the gleaming teeth
everything they had always wanted
but were afraid to speak of,

lifted loincloths and peeked,
loved and beat the help alternately,
as required. There were parks
now on the islands where the vines

had been chastened and the trees
pruned. But inside the Masters,
the overgrowth burgeoned out
of control into endless expanses

of troubled dreams. You cannot
imagine their suffering (though
they lived long and were not sick),
nor their despair. Yet daguerreotypes
were made in which the Master
and his family were luminous
and impeccable with all
their brass buttons, the servants

shadows that broke off
like black lightning and fetched
things from the margins of the frame.
Bats caught in gauze curtains.

And the terror bled out over silver bowls
of floating rose petals.
In the background the fruits
grew heavy on the branches

and if you gaze at the photo
long enough you will see them drop
to the ground and rot, ooze nectar
and be covered with wasps.

Stay longer still and you will see
the grand costumes stiffen
and stand by themselves, empty,
echoing bird cries and the wind

tunneling through the immaculate sleeves.
The jungle grows up through them.
Vines invade the manor house
and the well scums over. Finally

the statues fall over by themselves
and the children play on them as if
they had never been more than piles of stones.

The Torturer's Apprentice

Almost a man now,
he used to shudder
when the old man
slipped hatpin under fingernail
but now he's got
the master's calm,
the seducer's whiskey drift
to ply his subject
to give up his neighbor, tease
from him how many,
where and when.
Next month he'll have his first,
no more dabbing the old man's brow
with a cool towel,
no more sopping up the blood,
spraying air-freshener
to mask the lingering stink
of fear and anguish.
They've saved a little nun
for him, some dear thing
who still believes
that deep down people
are good.
We don't have to do this, Sister,
he'll say,
like a doctor, like a priest,
like he who giveth more
than you ever wanted.
Tell me
what I want to know

and I'll send you to God
with a single bullet in the nape.
You do not want
to finish this poem.
You do not want
to know who writes the check.
You do not want to know the fugitive self
you've sent down there,
where people do those things.
Where people do those things.

IV

ANSWERING ADORNO

Homage to Pound

There is a wine-red glow in the shallows,
A tin flash in the sun-dazzle.
Ezra Pound, Canto II

Young men in black shirts,
     knife of sun on bandolier straps
       tooth-light swagger
Of temporary immortality
    They will not
       melt in the rain, nor,
You thought,
    would your Jesus be foot-hung
       from a lamp post.
Where'd you lose your Virgil, at the fork?
    Ride the she-wolf into town
       to that hysterical
Historical saloon
    where hearts are tanned
       and blackened like jerky.
Wish you hadn't done that. We shod
    your sleek horse and groomed him,
       rode him in our tweed and corduroy
Through generations,
    let him show up in our cells
       like luminous fish in a plague tide.
Mad? How about *guilty*
    which leaves us with **Art**
       as no religion
No transformer
    but a shuck-and-jive man with a bone.

Let not my left brain
know what my right is writing. Hitler

wore Wagner like silk, Goethe like a veil
but you ate poetry
uncooked, fist by bloody fist.

Image-makers let us sell used cars together
with our craft.
Let us all go wash ourselves in the Ganges.

Conversion

The fire chief's daughter led them, Trip and Stumble,
to the boathouse, these brown, brown boys,
showed them the fire she kept, smoldering in a Bible.

Let them touch Bethesda moonwet in the bramble,
took them swollen, healed them pink and coy,
the fire chief's daughter led them, Trip and Stumble.

She heated them, then made them humble,
made them ache and then with plot and ploy,
showed them the fire she kept, smoldering in a Bible

to get them back again, these goat-rank bundles,
make them insane, then sweet with joy,
the fire chief's daughter led them, Trip and Stumble.

She dragged homeward, sopped and rumpled,
thighs weak and jellied from the roil,
showed them the fire she kept, smoldering in a Bible

to save their souls from certain stifle,
from the schoolmarm's righteous nightsoil,
the fire chief's daughter led them, Strip and Stumble,
showed them the fire she kept, smoldering in a Bible.

Something to Get Him Through

He talked about the skin on the inside of her arms, her neck, the way her hair smelled, and how one day when driving in the desert she stripped down to her slip, put her fine feet up on the dash, tilted her head back and slept. And the day she picked him up at the airport wearing only a t-shirt. She had been in prison for five years for something she could not possibly have done, was tortured regularly, raped, made to drink piss. Her huge soft eyes. *If you love someone enough they will heal. This is what we think. Everyone has done this, no?* His hands were shaking.

She began first saying things so cruel he thought she must have read his fears in the night when he was sleeping. Things to break him, kill him, make him drink acid. And without provocation. He stayed with her. He stayed. But she was so afraid he'd leave her she waited up for him one night when he came home later than usual and hit him in the face with a wrench when he opened the door. He almost lost an eye. He threw her out.

She came back. Would stand outside his apartment with her head hung, her large-curled, blue-black hair shrouding her face, the huge eyes burning through. He took her back. The cruelty began again, he threw her out. They did this three times and then he moved away to be rid of her. He tried other lovers but they knew he was broken and they went away. At the end of however much time—did he say ten years—he was free of her. When the heart lets go, the mind becomes glib. This is what he said to me: *I understood finally that because she had been so violated for what she did not do, she felt compelled to commit the crime.* His hands were shaking.

Critical Theory

A professor came to our village last year to study our dialect. He was fond of saying that words only related to other words and not to things in the world, and that everything written was a kind of playful lie. A game. He did not explain how, with such a belief, he could have any faith in his own books, which were numerous and widely read. I did not have a chance to question him deeply because this is what happened.

"You mean," said the village chief, "that bread does not mean bread?"
"No."
This answer so annoyed the village chief that he locked the professor in a cell underneath the main jail, the place reserved for the worst of criminals. I protested that this was harsh treatment for mere foolishness but he silenced me with a look.

The professor was fed irregularly and then only a crust of stale bread and some water. Each night the village chief would go down to the cell which was so dark that no light reached it, even in the day time, and he would say to the professor, "Well, does bread mean bread yet?" Or, "Does stone mean stone?"

And the professor, still thinking it a game, would say something like, "No, bread has come to mean, for example, *money,* or, at best, an archaic signifier for spiritual sustenance, as in *manna from heaven,* or, *daily bread.* And then he would grin and the village chief would go away, his jaw set.

But at the end of nine months when the professor had begun to eat his own lice, when finally a piece of bread was thrust through the slot in the door, he snatched it and stuffed it into his mouth full of bleeding gums as if he were stanching a wound. When finally he had begun to shriek and beat his head against the wall until blood ran into his eyes, he was prepared to say that bread was again bread and stone, stone. The chief gave him back his clothes and passport and fed him some dried goat.

Answering Adorno

To write poetry after Auschwitz is barbaric.

—Theodore Adorno

Since you doomed poetry nothing has changed.
People are the same, maybe worse.
In Bosnia they have raped by battalions,
nailed children to doors, rubbled fine old Europe
block by block, and the new evil pours into the deep cup
with the evil I have already seen, overflowing.
Convention demands that I mortify something.
My flesh. My heart. Any joy I might have
on this April day with forsythia suddenly everywhere
and the willows aching green gold.
Adorno, your words are like snow lingering
where shade and wind hold out against the sun.

Beast

I liked you
better
before that prim
lost thing
swam the moat
and transformed you:
preferred you
hunched
like Beethoven,
your hairy heart
raging,
pheromones
inscribing a nimbus
around you
within which circumference
foxgloves opened
and a rank perfume
trailed.
I preferred
your class resentments,
rusted earring,
your admonitions
about the east wing
where all your pain
is scrimshawed
on the skeletons
of traveling evangelists.
What was it?
Her sweet flesh,
clear eyes? You

became a prissy jock,
cliff-jawed
with cap-toothed gawp
and dutchboy coif,
knees gone raw with kneeling.
And wouldn't even *you,*
little lost one,
miss finishing school,
prefer his howling,
and throwing pianos
downstairs
to this simp
perched on the edge
of a velvet stool
with a teacup,
thinking
which word
to leave out
of the next sentence
to avoid offending?
Wouldn't you
prefer
the beast
hunched over you,
your claws
deep in his chest pelt,
vise-thighed
around his hips,
drop of sweat
hanging
from the tip
of his nose.

Falling

*To think clearly
what I need
is a pig and an angel.*
—Charles Simic

They are shackled to one another. No,
the pig wears the angel
and after tenure,
the angel wears the pig or is it
the other way round?

Deny the pig at the angel's expense:
*he who thrusts his pig into darkness
        shall soil his wings.*
And there is the pig who hides his angel
because he has spent so long
in the company of pigs
his wings have atrophied.
They ache every time a wind blows
from Heaven.

The angel knows when to let the pig speak
and the pig knows never
to try to speak like an angel
but this is only because
of the way minds are wound and set.
Sometimes one will wake in the night
and find the other sleeping.
He will say: *I know you. I can
see your thoughts*

and then for a brief time there is no difference
between pig and angel.

But then morning again
and the pig wakes from a nightmare
of being flung out of heaven
into a great frozen sty
and the angel wakes from a vision of lemon groves
and then the old rounds,
the old habits,
the same words aching from the throat.

Ars Poetica

I

Another day gone and not prepared for death.
The trains keep me up all night
and insomniacs sit red-eyed in the windows,
drowned in amber. All that is missing
are the uniforms with gold epaulets,
decanters of brandy, unscheduled stops
and the unbathed revolutionaries
kissing us with their garlic-clove teeth.
The engines grouse in the switchyard,
run their lurid spotlights over the new graffiti.
Do we cry out on the turns, steel against steel?
Squirrel away wisdom: thy pantry is thy comfort
and stock the corpse boat well.
I am old enough to have outlived two lovers,
and the president, for once,
is younger than me. And randier
(although that's been disputed).
I just can't keep up with the times.
Those bonded by extruded navels protest
they have been marginalized,
but I say these little anomalies
are what drive us to greatness   look at Richard III.
We're all tangled together down in the muck
and the lotus roots.
Our new poems are bouquets of wide open eyes,
eggwhite from too long in holes
of our own imagining.
The light like a knife in the brain.

II

I can no longer abide the self-serious,
the voice that says
My pain is important
and probably deeper than yours
so listen up. Nor the establishing shot
in nature: we sit under a pear tree
and the grass turns its dull side to the wind.
Well, maybe the second line, but why not
We sit under a bouquet of chainsaws?
If poetry is meant
to discover the world
I cannot be happy with sitting under a tree
even if the other half of *We*
is anatomically astonishing
and butt-naked. Help me, please,
to the place where the best of me
culminates in a wave
and becomes a word. Or the worst,
whatever makes the poem.
Let there be no more schools and movements
and especially let there be
no more Romantiks
hoarding the last cubic yard of pastoral ground
in the shadows of the great mirrored buildings.
Let there be instead
a balloon rising over the child's slapped hand
or the burnt
places on the ground where the carnival was
and gypsies pissed.
And let there be some reason to speak

words to one another
even if it is through the peacock's tail of our lies.

III.

We think we are talking to the others at our table
but our voices are pitched high enough
to be heard by the great absence himself.
Who looks over our shoulders as we write?
Besides, our secrets are all known,
we keep articulating them, honing them,
until our utterance is "pure."
This, all our lives, so that we can say to death
(who is busy)
I have lived,
I have done these things,
I have done evil, for which I am famous,
and some good, which is unknown.
And love.
Well. I have done my best.
This must be said quickly on the last day
in as few words as possible.
But they must be the right words.

Town Meeting

They were defecating in public, he said,
and someone else said,
copulating, too,
and I thought, how many, a thousand?
All the homeless there are copulating in public? What a vision.
And then someone said,
not all the homeless
and we breathed easier,
only fifteen or so, and I thought
that's still a lot of them to be doing that in public
and by the time we were done
it was apparent
there had been only one each:
one copulation, one defecation,
and then someone else said,
you don't have to be homeless to do that.

Notes

Blues for Unemployed Mercenaries:

Under apartheid, the SA Special Branch hired snipers who would freeze water in bullet molds then load the ice bullets into shell casings with an ammo loader. Since ice melts in body heat the technique was perfectly antiforensic.

Homage to Pound:

When poet Robert Mezey went to visit Pound in St. Elizabeths he asked the great man to read some of his new poems. Pound said (and I paraphrase) "Surely, but I have to warn you that I give everything first to Mr. Weiss over there to see if it's worth reading." Then Pound nodded across the room at Mr. Weiss, a waxen catatonic. From this Mezey concluded that Pound was completely sane and therefore responsible for his actions.

DOUG ANDERSON, a Vietnam vet, holds an M.A. in playwriting from the University of Arizona, and has taught creative writing at a number of universities, most recently Pitzer College. He also frequently teaches in the William Joiner Center's summer workshops at The University of Massachusetts-Boston. His first book of poetry, *The Moon Reflected Fire* (Alice James, 1994), won the Kate Tufts Discovery Award for Poetry. In addition to three books of poetry, he has published fiction and criticism, and his work has been praised by such poets as Bruce Weigl, Daniel Halpern, Thomas Lux, Garrett Hongo, and Maxine Kumin. His critical writings have appeared in *The New York Times, The London Times Literary Supplement,* and *The Boston Globe.*

CURBSTONE PRESS, INC.

is a non-profit publishing house dedicated to literature that reflects a commitment to social change, with an emphasis on contemporary writing from Latino, Latin American and Vietnamese cultures. Curbstone presents writers who give voice to the unheard in a language that goes beyond denunciation to celebrate, honor and teach. Curbstone builds bridges between its writers and the public – from inner-city to rural areas, colleges to community centers, children to adults. Curbstone seeks out the highest aesthetic expression of the dedication to human rights and intercultural understanding: poetry, testimonies, novels, stories, and children's books.

This mission requires more than just producing books. It requires ensuring that as many people as possible know about these books and read them. To achieve this, a large portion of Curbstone's schedule is dedicated to arranging tours and programs for its authors, working with public school and university teachers to enrich curricula, reaching out to underserved audiences by donating books and conducting readings and community programs, and promoting discussion in the media. It is only through these combined efforts that literature can truly make a difference.

Curbstone Press, like all non-profit presses, depends on the support of individuals, foundations, and government agencies to bring you, the reader, works of literary merit and social significance which might not find a place in profit-driven publishing channels, and to bring the authors and their books into communities across the country. Our sincere thanks to the many individuals who support this endeavor and to the following businesses, foundations and government agencies: Connecticut Commission on the Arts, Connecticut Arts Endowment Fund, Connecticut Humanities Council, Daphne Seyboldt Culpeper Foundation, J.M. Kaplan Fund's Furthermore program, Eric Mathieu King Fund, Lannan Foundation, Lawson-Valentine Foundation, John D. and Catherine T. MacArthur Foundation, National Endowment for the Arts, Open Society Institute, and the Puffin Foundation.

Please support Curbstone's efforts to present the diverse voices and views that make our culture richer. Tax-deductible donations can be made by check or credit card to:
Curbstone Press, 321 Jackson Street, Willimantic, CT 06226
phone: (860) 423-5110   fax: (860) 423-9242
www.curbstone.org